JAMES CAGNEY

JAMES CAGNEY

IN THE SPOTLIGHT

GALLEY PRESS

A Division of Mayflower Books, Inc.
New York, New York 10022

ISBN: 8317—1147-7

Library of Congress Catalog Card Number: 80-82358

PHOTO CREDITS

Museum of Modern Art
Pg. 9, 12, 13, 14, 15, 16, 17, 18, 20, 21, 23, 24, 25, 26, 27, 30, 33, 34, 35, 36, 37, 38, 39, 41, 42, 45, 51, 56, 59, 65, 70, 71, 75, 80, 81, 83, 85, 86, 88, 89, 94, 95, 96, 97, 98, 99, 100 & 101, 103.

UPI
Pg. 8, 19, 22, 23, 28, 29, 40, 43, 44, 46, 47 (2 pics.), 48, 49, 52, 53, 55, 58, 63, 64, 67, 68, 69, 72, 73, 77, 78, 79, 82, 84, 87, 90, 91, 92, 102, 104, 105, 106, 107, 108, 109, 110, 111, 112, 113, 114, 115, 116, 118.

Hy Simon
Pg. 10, 31, 32, 33, 50, 54, 57, 60, 61, 62, 66, 93, 117, 119.

NCNY
Pg. 74.

CONTENTS

1
JAMES CAGNEY: HOLLYWOOD'S TOUGH GUY   8

2
THE FILMS OF JAMES CAGNEY   120

JAMES CAGNEY:

HOLLYWOOD'S TOUGH GUY

James Cagney, age 14.

(Right) Publicity photograph, 1930.

James Cagney: Hollywood's Tough Guy

James Cagney is an actor best known to his countless fans as *the* tough guy; more often than not, his inimitable fast-talking staccato voice telling some mug where to get off is what most movie fans remember about his career. Comedian Bob Hope once defined a Cagney love scene as "when he lets the other guy live." James Cagney is, and has always been, a tough, principled man who has never been a pushover. But it would be a mistake to assume that his toughness reflects anything more than one small aspect of this multi-talented man. Cagney once said: "I am not the characters I

play. I believe that in order to do anything well, you must have perspective, a certain amount of objectivity, of detachment. This is necessary in order to give a clear portrait of a character. If I were a 'tough guy,' I couldn't play one even as well as I hope to do."

James Cagney is actually a gentle man who established his roots in show business as a vaudeville song and dance man, who successfully segued into motion pictures, and who became one of America's most respected citizens. He is a man who has not only mastered several crafts, but one who has applied his acting, painting, and poetic abilities to the betterment of all. He cherishes the land and has been active as an ecologist for many years. Above all, he is a man who considers country living, close friendships, and his relationship with his wife and children as the most precious of his life's rewards.

During James Cagney's 50-year career, in which he appeared on the live stage, in over 70 films, and on radio and television, acting has only been a job — an enjoyable and rewarding job, but nonetheless, only a means to an end. Early in his career, he established the goal of one day retiring to a farm. His dream became a reality, but only after many years of perserverance.

James Cagney's parents were immigrants. James Francis Cagney, Sr., and Carolyn Nelson came to America in the late 1890s and were married. He was a stout Irishman; she was half Irish, half Norwegian. At first they lived in a small flat on Eighth Street and Avenue D in New York City. James, Sr., worked as a bartender, then owned his own saloon. Carolyn tended to the needs of her growing family. Harry was the first born. James, Jr., their second child, was born on July 17, 1899. When Jimmy was a year old, his family moved to Yorkville, an Upper East Side neighborhood. Today, Yorkville is a relatively peaceful area, but at the turn of the century, the neighborhood was anything but that. The area was primarily inhabited by immigrants; severe unrest and unemployment were prevalent. Street fighting was common, and law was based more on concepts of retribution than on a belief in government.

In contrast to their neighborhood, the Cagney home life was nearly ideal. Edward and

With Mae Clarke in *The Public Enemy* (1931).

Director William Wellman (c.) gets ready to shoot a scene from *The Public Enemy* (1931).
Cagney is at right.

(Left) With Jean Harlow in *The Public Enemy* (1931).

William were born, bringing the family total to six. James, Sr., believed that joviality was the key to good living. His early morning routine, for example, was to kiss his children, prepare himself for work, kiss his wife Carrie before leaving, don his bowler hat, bless himself, and go off to his job— all in high spirits. Jimmy once described his father's end-of-the-day routine: "Say, you know that business I have of tipping the girl on the chin with my fist to show her I like her?...I got that from my father. He used to do that to us kids when we were young, me and my brothers...He would

On the set of *The Public Enemy* (1931). Cagney flanked by co-star Jean Harlow and Edward Woods (r.).

walk up to us and stand like a prize fighter with his fists up. Then he would give us a light tap on the chin. Then he would kiss us. We used to like for him to do that."

Although Carolyn had many maternal duties, she was always the source of emotional support for her sons. Jimmy recalls that her firm hand always steered her children in constructive directions and that he and his brothers stayed clear of crime primarily because "we had a mother to answer to. If any of us got out of line, she just belted us. We loved her profoundly and

Publicity photograph.

our driving force was to do what she wanted because we knew how much it meant to her."

Early on, Jimmy wanted to be a farmer, and Mrs. Cagney encouraged him and took him to lectures on the environment. "She was one of those gals who had the good sense to know that every-

body had to go his own way. She had wonderfully practical ways of showing her love and concern for us."

In 1914, while attending Stuyvesant High School at Fifteenth Street and First Avenue, Jimmy also began contributing to the family income:

With Edward G. Robinson (c.) and director Al Green (for. r.) on the set of *Smart Money* (1931).

(Right) Filming *Smart Money* (1931), with Noel Francis (standing) and Edward G. Robinson (l.).

"I feel sorry for the kid who has too cushy a time of it. Suddenly, he has to come face to face with the realities of life without any Papa and Mama to do his thinking for him." After school hours, he worked as a copy boy for the *New York Sun*. Later, he wrapped parcels for Wanamaker's department store. Also during his high school years, he worked at a pool hall, as a bellhop, as an employee of the Hudson River Day Line tour boat, and more.

In his last year of high school, Jimmy applied to an agricultural school. He was accepted, but was informed that his admission would be delayed for one year. During this interim year, 1917-1918, he enrolled in Columbia University. Six months into his studies, he was drafted by the U.S. Army. Before he was shipped overseas, however, the Great War in Europe ended, and he was again free to continue his education. But this was not to

With director Frank Capra (l.) Darryl F. Zanuck (r.), and Jack Warner (r.) in Hollywood, 1932.

be the case. James, Sr., passed away in late 1918 during a flu epidemic, and with his mother pregnant with sister Jeanne and his brothers all in school, young Cagney became the major breadwinner of the family.

When he was not working, Cagney was encouraged by his mother to get out of the house and pursue his many varied interests. It was during this period in his life that he became the runner-up for the New York State lightweight boxing championship; he became a star catcher for a community baseball team that was good enough to go on

Press photograph, 1933.

Chatting with actress Sharon Lynn at the Beverly Wilshire, 1933.

an exhibition tour; and he also became involved in something that would ultimately evolve into his livelihood—community theater.

Cagney's first acting role came as a result of his brother Harry falling ill just prior to his performing in a Lenox Hill Settlement House drama club production. Cagney, who painted scenery for the club, was suddenly asked to take Harry's place. "That was my real introduction to acting, but that was by no means the reason for my going into show business."

Cagney continued as an amateur performer until 1919 when he saw *Every Sailor* at Keith's Eighty-Sixth Street Theatre. The show consisted of six men in "drag" performing chorus line numbers. When they needed a replacement, Cagney grabbed the job. He couldn't dance, but for paying work, he'd do anything. His salary was $35 a week, "a mountain of money for me in those worrisome days. That is how I began to learn dancing—as a chorus girl. I faked it to begin with. I would stand in the entrance, catch the real dancers, and steal their steps. In all the dancing shows I did, I learned by watching."

Mrs. Cagney welcomes Jimmy home from New York, 1933.

Arriving in New York after filming *Hard to Handle* (1933).

At the Montmarte Cafe, Hollywood, 1933. Left to right: Cagney, Mrs. Cagney, radio singer Bobby Arnst, Boots Mallory (Mrs. William Cagney), and Cagney's brother William.

After *Every Sailor* closed, Cagney got a job as a stock exchange runner; then he heard about a casting call for a chorus boy in the Broadway show *Pitter Patter* and auditioned for it. Cagney won a small part and opened in the play at the Longacre Theater in September of 1920, where his aptitude for dancing began to show itself, and he was soon moved from the chorus to specialty dances. Cagney, for all his good fortune, was not satisfied with a $35 a week salary, so he took on extra jobs that increased his earnings to $55 a week, $40 of which he sent home to his mother.

Also appearing in *Pitter Patter* was Frances Willard Vernon (called "Bill" by her friends), a woman Cagney took an immediate and strong liking to, and whom he married when the show closed. The newlyweds formed their own vaudeville act called "Vernon and Nye." During the next

Vitch (r.), caricaturist at Hollywood's Brown Derby, caricatured by Cagney, 1933.

With columnist Walter Winchell (r.), 1933.

few years, they toured with the act and also worked together and separately in anything that would pay their bills: Cagney appeared with "Midge Miller and Her Boy Friends" as one of the "boyfriends" and with the Jaffe Troupe of actors; they worked together in *Lew Field's Ritz Girls of 1922,* and later, in *Lew Field's Snapshots of 1923.*

In 1924, the Cagneys traveled to Los Angeles to find work and to introduce Jimmy to Bill's mother. Their reception at the Hollywood studios was less than encouraging, so they traveled back to New York, where they opened a dance studio (which ultimately failed) and continued touring with their vaudeville act.

During a six-month period in 1925, Cagney replaced Cary Grant in the vaudeville team of 'Parker, Rand and Leach.' (Grant was still known as Archie Leach at the time.) Years later, Cagney spoke about this period of his life: "[After the "Parker, Rand and Cagney" tour, I] worked in a wide variety of acts even though I was taking a

good chance of being fired—as I was occasionally—because I had exaggerated my abilities. In the midst of all that hardship of jobs gained, jobs lost, jobs deferred, jobs lousy, jobs few, there was always the wonder of my 'Bill.' [Marrying] her in 1922 [was] absolutely the smartest thing I ever did in the whole course of my life, and I am still crazy about this lady after nearly 60 years of marriage."

By the end of 1925, their luck changed. Maxwell Anderson's *Outside Looking In* was casting, and Cagney rushed to audition for the role of "Little Red." "There were only two actors in New York with red hair, Alan Bunce and myself. I assume I got the part because my hair was redder than Alan's." The show ran for four months.

In 1927, the Cagneys worked together in a comedy routine in *Lonesome Manor.* Later that year, Cagney heard about a part in George Abbott and Philip Dunning's play *Broadway.* He auditioned and was signed to a run-of-the-show contract for what he hoped would be the starring role

Cagney and Wynne Gibson rehearse some of the old steps, 1933.

Mr. and Mrs. Cagney, 1933.

At home, 1933.

in the London version of the show. Instead, he ended up as understudy to Lee Tracy, the star of the New York production.

Cagney next found work in *Women Go On Forever*, a play featuring Mary Boland. It was during this time that the Cagneys opened a small dancing school in Elizabeth, New Jersey. "It was one of my great life mistakes." Both the school and the show soon closed.

Cagney next danced in *The Grand Street Follies of 1928* and then *The Grand Street Follies of 1929*, both successful revues.

In October 1929, Cagney appeared in George Kelly's *Maggie the Magnificent*. Also in the cast was a young girl named Joan Blondell, with whom he would perform on many occasions throughout his career. "I must say I noted at the time that she had a perfectly beautiful body—something my

With "Bill", his wife, at home, 1934.

bride knows I've said a number of times."

In fact, Cagney's next appearance in 1929 was on stage in *Penny Arcade* with Joan Blondell. *Penny Arcade* is a story about the children of a woman who owns an arcade and their involvement in rum-running. Cagney played Harry Delano, one of the two sons. The play was well received by the critics but closed after only a three-week run. Entertainer Al Jolson, however,

had enjoyed the play so much that he purchased the motion picture rights, and he wanted Cagney and Blondell to recreate their roles on the screen. For Cagney, it not only meant three weeks of guaranteed salary, it also meant a trip to Hollywood. He stayed 31 years.

Sinner's Holiday (1930) became the film title for *Penny Arcade*; it took 21 days to film, and Cagney's salary was $400 a week. He really did not

At home, 1934.

(Right) Petting his dog on the patio of his California home, 1934.

And Cagney later remarked: "My very first impression of Hollywood was the same as with any other town I had encountered in vaudeville—just a place to do your job. But after a while, I began to realize how sadly obsessed these Hollywood people were with their careers."

When *Sinner's Holiday* completed filming, its producer, Warner Bros'., asked Cagney to appear in *Doorway to Hell* (1930), starring Lew Ayers. It was Warner Bros., first major gangster film of the 1930s. It is the story of a big-time beer baron (Ayers) who tries to quit the rackets. He turns his bootlegging business over to his lieutenant (Cagney), is eventually betrayed by his wife, and is killed while attempting to avenge the murder of his brother. This picture stressed not only social realism, but also the doom awaiting all gangsters. It also marked the first appearance, albeit a minor, supporting role, by Cagney as a gangster—a prelude to the characterization of a tough guy with a cocky manner, a New York accent, and a captivating but dangerous grin that would become his trademark in the future.

"While we were shooting, Warners came to me with a long-term contract. But even then I didn't think this was going to be my future."

In 1931, Cagney made a very brief appearance in *Other Men's Women* (1931), a railroad melodrama that starred Grant Withers and Mary Astor. *The Millionaire* (1931) presented Cagney with the shortest role of his career, a two-minute scene with its star, George Arliss, in which Cagney, as a fast-talking insurance salesman, must sell a policy to Arliss. It was in this role that the high-pitched, staccato manner of speech that would come to be identified with Cagney first emerged.

Cagney's next role was in *The Public Enemy* (1931), a story about two street pals who rise from impoverished childhoods to become wealthy, unrepentant Chicago gangsters. By the end of the film, both have been killed to remind the viewers that "crime does not pay." *The Public Enemy* is considered by many film buffs to be the most famous gangster film of all time and the film that firmly established Cagney as a major star of the genre. Oddly enough, Edward Woods was originally cast to play the role of the boisterous and tough Tom Powers, and Cagney was to play

expect to stay in the picture business for long; all the big stars out there, he recalls, felt certain that their good luck was only temporary and sooner or later, it would run out. "I'm not going to buy anything I can't take back on the train with me," was something he remembers Clark Gable saying.

With Bette Davis in *Jimmy the Gent* (1934).

the more subdued Matt Doyle, but three days into the shooting, producer Darryl Zanuck and director William Wellman agreed that the roles were miscast and should be reversed.

The Public Enemy was filmed in just over three weeks and contains one of James Cagney's most memorable scenes—he pushes half a grapefruit into Mae Clark's face. The film also featured many scenes with lots of bullets bouncing off walls, cars, and sidewalks. Real bullets, fired by a trained World War I machine gunner, were used in the filming. Cagney commented later that several

Publicity photograph, *Devil Dogs of the Air* (1935).

times he was nearly killed.

The Public Enemy cost $151,000 to film. It made more than ten times that amount at the box office and became one of Hollywood's first big grossing, low-budget pictures.

"After *Public Enemy* was released, Warners gave me star billing, which was pleasant enough, but hardly compensation for the lack of compensation. I kept grinding the pictures out, working at a swift tempo, and seeing everywhere about me the rough-handed treatment of actors by management. Actors were considered to be expendable

As "Brick" Davis in *G-Men* (1935).

material, just like props or make up. I watched this, and I was to remember."

In an effort to capitalize on the success of *The Public Enemy* and another hit gangster movie, *Little Caesar* (First National, 1931) starring Edward G. Robinson, Warner Bros. rushed to team Cagney

and Robinson in *Smart Money* (1931). This movie is yet another view of big city crime and was Cagney and Robinson's only collaboration. It is the story of Nick "The Barber" Venizelos (Robinson) and his pal Jack (Cagney) who leave their small town existence to set up a gambling house and make it big in the city.

Blonde Crazy (1931) co-starred Joan Blondell, and in Cagney's words, he played a "red-hot bellhop loaded for larceny." The story was about two con artists on a cross-country spree. This picture was actually Cagney and Blondell's fifth venture together, but *Blonde Crazy* was considered their real beginning as a starring team. *The New York Times* called the film "lively and cleverly acted."

In 1931, Cagney's brother William arrived in California for a vacation. He looked much like his older brother and even appeared in a few films, but his heart wasn't in acting, however, so the brothers agreed that William would become Cagney's business manager.

Cagney's next film was *Taxi!* (1931). It was the first film in which he appeared for Warner Bros. under the terms of a new contract signed by Jack Warner in response to a Cagney walkout. This contract practically tripled Cagney's weekly salary and dramatically alerted others in the industry to unrest among studio contract players. "I did an entire series of walkouts over the years. I walked out because I depended on the studio heads to keep their word on this and that and when the promise was not kept, my only recourse was to deprive them of my services. I'd go back east until we had some kind of understanding. I'm glad to say I never walked out in the middle of a picture. Moreover, I got solid support from people in my profession...It wasn't until some of us began to do a little walking out that the studio's total dictatorship over talent began to diminish."

Taxi! co-starred Loretta Young as Cagney's girlfriend, was directed by Roy Del Ruth, and also marked the first screen appearance by a young actor, George Raft. The script put Cagney on the "right" side of the law as the leader of a small band of cab drivers fighting to stay independent of the mob. *Taxi!* is remembered not only for bringing Cagney and Raft together, but for showcasting Cagney as a dancer for the first time on film. He also had to learn to drive a car for the part—something he had never bothered to do.

Director Howard Hawks's most obscure work might be *The Crowd Roars* (1932), a drama about a road racer's compulsion to win. Cagney

On location for *The Irish in Us* (1935).

On the set of *A Midsummer Night's Dream* (1935).

Rehearsing for *A Midsummer Night's Dream* (1935) Left to right: Joe E. Brown, Mickey Rooney, Dewey Robinson, Arthur Treacher, Frank McHugh, Otis Harlan, Cagney, Hugh Herbert, director Max Reinhardt, and dialogue director Stanley Logan.

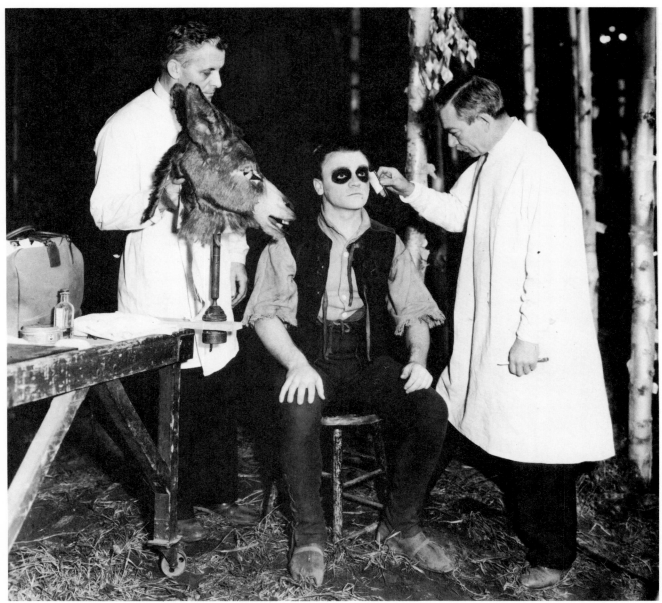

Being made up for the part of Bottom in *A Midsummer Night's Dream* (1935).

plays Joe Green, a driver whose ambitions cause a friend's death during a race. The friend was played by Frank McHugh, who would later appear in many Cagney films. "After our first day of shooting on *The Crowd Roars,* Frank and I shared a suite at the Santa Barbara Hotel. We were just get-

ting acquainted. We stayed up the entire night and talked. Which will give you some idea of the many things we had in common."

Winner Take All (1932) was a fight picture that highlighted a boxer's dilemma: choosing between a lovely, plain girl (Marion Nixon) or one of

Rehearsing for *A Midsummer Night's Dream* (1935), with Joe E. Brown (l.), Mickey Rooney (seated, c.), and director Max Reinhardt (seated r.).

high society (Virginia Bruce). In preparatrion for his role as Jim Kane, Cagney trained for three weeks in Palm Springs, California, with former bantam and flyweight boxer Harvey Perry.

Because of further contract negotiations, Cagney left Hollywood in early 1932, but he returned in October of that year and starred in Mervyn Leroy's comedy-drama, *Hard to Handle* (1933), at a substantial pay increase. In the story, Cagney plays a fast-talking promoter named Lefty Merrill. Lefty has sponsored a marathon dance contest and plans to abscond with the entrance

fees, but his partner does so first, leaving Lefty to handle the angry crowd that is waiting for an explanation. The picture was well received and marked another plain script and hasty production made special by Cagney's appearance in it.

Picture Snatcher (1933), a movie filmed in only 15 days, starred Cagney as a reformed crook who is hired by a newspaper to take candid, embarrassing photographs of public figures. The film co-starred Ralph Bellamy. "One day...I was walking through [rehearsing] a scene with Ralph, laying out what I was going to do. I stood outside a door waiting for my cue, bounced in, and went to his desk. We did our words, there was a phone call, then some more words. Suddenly I heard our director Lloyd Bacon yell, 'Cut—print it.' I said, 'Hey, you; I was rehearsing.' 'It looked fine from here,' he said!"

The Mayor of Hell (1933) is an exciting drama set in a boys' reform school. Patsy Gargan (Cagney) is a crook who rids the school of its overbearing administrator, becomes popular with the students, and has a romance with the school nurse (Madge Evans). One day he reverts to his old tough ways, kills a rival gangster, and flees across state lines to avoid arrest. The tyrannical former administrator returns to the school and cruelly punishes the boys, but he is foiled by Patsy once again.

Footlight Parade (1933) is one of Warner Bros.' all-time great musical extravaganzas and provided James Cagney with his first opportunity to sing and dance throughout a motion picture. Cagney plays Chester Kent, a law-abiding, manic, hard working producer of live stage shows that appeared in conjunction with films in theaters throughout the country. The picture co-starred Dick Powell, Ruby Keeler, Joan Blondell, and Frank McHugh. The dance numbers were all staged by master showman Busby Berkeley.

Footlight Parade has always been one of Cagney's favorite films. Years later, he remarked that the picture "was one of those flubby musical incredibilities, pure fantasy all the way, but it gave the song and dance people a chance to be employed. Little Ruby Keeler danced her heart out, and she knew what she was doing. And as for Dick Powell—people never realized what a good voice that boy had, and a lot of nice things to go with it. I

Trying out new kitchenware, 1935.

(Left) Publicity photograph. *Frisco Kid* (1935).

was terribly fond of this nice, nice guy all the years I knew him. When that throat cancer took him, we were devastated because he was a rare one."

Lady Killer (1933) turned Cagney back into a tough guy in the role of racketeer Dan Quigley who accidentally becomes a Hollywood star. The intent of this farcical picture, which again paired Cagney with Mae Clarke, was to poke fun at Hollywood where former crooks supposedly *had*

In conversation with close friend Pat O'Brien, 1935.

made it big. But, the movie was poorly paced; it suffered from a weak script and made no real statement.

The 1934 comedy production of *Jimmy the Gent* starred Cagney as Jimmy Corrigan, a tough business agent/con artist whose racket is providing fake heirs to huge fortunes. The major female role was played by a relatively new face in Hollywood—Bette Davis. The film passed with little notice.

By this time, Cagney was fed up with shallow gangster parts. In fact, when he learned about

Cagney and Mae Clarke during a break in the filming of *Great Guy* (1936).

Warner Bros.' plan to cast him in *Jimmy the Gent,* he prepared a surprise for director Michael Curtiz as a form of protest: "I had my head shaved down right to the skull except for a little top knot in front, and I had the make up man put scars all over the back of my head. The opening shot was of my back to the camera, with all those scars in sharp focus. The phone rings, I turn around to speak—and Mike Curtiz damn near fainted when he saw that shaved head."

He Was Her Man (1934) featured a romance between a former prostitute (Joan Blondell) and a

As Terry Rooney in *Something to Sing About* (1937).

Typical Cagney pose.

Aboard his boat.

(Left) Roller-skating with Ira Gershwin (l.) and Joan Crawford, 1937.

safe cracker (Cagney) who is on the run from vengeful rivals. It was their seventh and last picture together, and it was received with little fanfare.

Here Comes the Navy (1934) is a comedy-drama about the hostility between a seaman and his superior officer, and it was the first of eight James Cagney — Pat O'Brien pictures. *Here Comes the Navy* was filmed on board the ill-fated *U.S.S. Arizona* and was nominated for Best Picture of 1934 by the Motion Picture Academy.

After appearing in a "bit part" in Frank

At a Hollywood Premier in the early 1930's.

Lloyd's *Mutiny on the Bounty* (1934) for MGM (a part so small it's unclear if he ever appeared in the final version of the film), Cagney starred as happy-go-lucky truck driver Eddie Kennedy in *The St. Louis Kid* (1934). As the story unfolds, the truck drivers' union calls a strike, but Eddie continues his Chicago-St. Louis run and is branded a "smart aleck scab." In retaliation for his defiance, he is framed for murder, but by the film's conclusion he is exonerated.

Cagney was unhappy about having to accept this part, but instead of protesting by shaving his

Leaving from New York on the *20th Century Limited,*
1938.

head, as he had for *Jimmy the Gent,* he tried something else. "By the time I was ready to do *The St.
Louis Kid,* I was so fed up with walking in and
punching people again and again that I had the
make up man wrap my hands in bandages. Instead of punching, I hit people between the eyes
with my forehead. I can still hear the reedy voice
of the film's producer: 'When are you going to
take those bandages off and start punching right?'
This gentleman rather failed to understand what I
was trying to do. In his book, I was simply trying to
foul up his living."

In the beginning of the 1930s, most actors
received two cents for every box-office dollar
taken in and were forced to work at least six days a
week. Cagney recalls: "They were squeezing as
much out of us as they could—twelve-hour days,
frequently working nights right through sun up.
This didn't bother the studio heads because they
were home with their families having dinner at the
appropriate hour."

Cagney felt that actors needed union representation, so when the Screen Actors Guild was
formed in 1934, he immediately joined. When it
became obvious that SAG was there to stay, the
studio bosses began to pit actors against each
other, sometimes by spreading false rumors of actors bad-mouthing their colleagues. Cagney recalls good friend Robert Montgomery saying at
the time: "Those unprincipled sons-of-bitches are

With the Dead End Kids in *Angels with Dirty Faces* (1938).

With his wife (c.), watching the Australian Davis Cup tennis squad practice, 1939.

going to do everything they can to keep us at odds with each other." Eventually, SAG grew large and powerful enough to influence the studios to work with them instead of against them.

It was also in 1934 that famed author Upton Sinclair campaigned as the Democratic candidate for Governor of California. Many major Hollywood studios opposed his election because of his overt liberalism, especially regarding the rights of actors and others in the creative end of filmmaking. The studios retaliated by funneling huge sums of money into the campaign coffer of Sinclair's opponent, incumbent governor Frank E. Merriam. Much of this money came from a controversial quasi-voluntary levy on studio workers' paychecks, which was the object of a rebellion led by Cagney and friend Jean Harlow. Sinclair was, nevertheless, defeated.

With Pat O'Brien at Ruby Foo's Vendome, 1939.

Statistics revealed that by 1935, James Cagney had entered the top ten players list in box-office popularity. "That kind of thing I found essentially meaningless. I never gave it a thought. Whatever was going on in my Hollywood life I regarded as completely transitory. I once saw a very well known playwright in a restaurant walking from table to table shaking hands and receiving congratulations. I thought it was very sad. He needed that support, all the praise and adulation. He needed it badly, sought it avidly. He savored every bit of that temporary eminence instead of just buckling down and furthering his job. That, I think, is what I did. Just going along, doing my job. Nothing more than that." (In addition to the adulation of fans, Cagney would also earn $147,167 in 1935—a large sum for the time.)

Cagney's first film of 1935 was *Devil Dogs of*

Mr. and Mrs. Robert Montgomery (l.) and the Cagneys attend the premiere of *Goodbye Mr. Chips,* 1939.

(Left) With Rosemary Lane in a scene from *The Oklahoma Kid* (1939).

the Air, the flying version of *Here Comes the Navy.* Cagney plays an arrogant stunt flyer, Tommy O'Toole, who competes for the affections of a waitress (Margaret Lindsay) against a Marine Flying Corps lieutenant (Pat O'Brien). Frank McHugh and Allen Jenkins appeared in the film and lent a slightly comic tone to the action, but *Devil Dogs of the Air* was a disappointment to most Cagney buffs and is remembered more for its exciting aerial sequences.

Next came *G-Men* (1935), in which Cagney again appears as a character on the right side of the law. This time he plays James "Brick" Davis, an honest lawyer who becomes a government special agent after an old college friend is gunned down by mobsters. Cagney proved to be as eminently believable playing an honest tough guy as he was when playing a dishonest one, and *G-Men*

started a new trend glorifying the lawmen instead of the law breakers. (This movie was re-issued in 1949 as part of the 25th anniversary celebration of the F.B.I.)

The Irish in Us (1935) was filmed in 18 days with a weak script and a low budget. Director Lloyd Bacon told his actors to "put in anything [you can] think up." The story is about a tightly-knit Irish family: Mary Gordon plays the mother; Pat O'Brien, the policeman brother; Frank McHugh, the fireman brother; and Cagney, the fight promoter brother. In the end, Cagney must replace his fighter in the ring. He wins the big fight, wins the girl (Olivia de Havilland), and all ends happily. This "B" picture, surprisingly, netted over $2 million, to the credit of its marvelous cast.

One of the more lavish Warner Bros. projects of the 1930s was *A Midsummer Night's Dream* (1935), in which Cagney played Bottom, the weaver. "A year before we did it," he later explained, "there had been a successful Hollywood Bowl presentation of the play directed by Max Reinhardt, and Warners' Hal Wallis decided to re-create it. I think he wanted to do something other than the knock 'em down-drag 'em outs we'd been doing for so long. Since he had the Warners stock company at hand to draw from—people like Joe E. Brown, Dick Powell, Frank McHugh, Olivia de Havilland, Victor Jory—he did it." The film was not acclaimed by the press, nor did it do well at the box office. The entire cast of the movie, however, believed in their American, contemporary version of the Elizabethan classic and was disappointed that so many viewers preferred the standard interpretation of it.

Frisco Kid (1935) had been sold to distributors before its shooting began. Unfortunately, little consideration was given to its artistic aspects. Cagney plays Bat Morgan, a Barbary Coast sailor who pushes his way to riches in San Francisco in the Gay Nineties. The film provided viewers with little more than barroom brawls and shootings.

Ceiling Zero (1935) was one of Cagney's finest roles; he plays Dizzy Davis, a flamboyant air mail pilot whose easygoing nature causes him to take too lightly the perilous weather conditions he must face while flying. During a mission, his irresponsible attitude causes the death of his buddy

Rehearsing a scene from *The Roaring Twenties* (1939).
Raoul Walsh, the director, in the foreground. Behind
him, Humphrey Bogart.

(Right) A helping hand for Judy Garland.

(Pat O'Brien). Later, he loses his own life as well.
The screenplay for *Ceiling Zero* was adapted by
playwright Frank Wead from his successful
Broadway play. Wead was a former naval aviator,
and the result was a very realistic film.

Cagney had now made five pictures in one

year, a violation of his Warner Bros. contract, so
he "walked away until they could make a better
arrangement. We [he and his brother William]
filed suit against them to rectify the inequities."

While the case underwent judicial review in
1936, Cagney surprised the industry by making a

At Paramount studios, 1930's, with Bing Crosby (l.) and Carole Lombard.

film for a new company, Grand National Pictures. The movie was *Great Guy* (1936). Cagney plays Johnny Cave, a good-natured, ex-fighter,who is now a meat inspector aiding the authorities in the uncovering of racketeering in the meat packing business. The film was shot on a small budget and the plot line was thin, but it did well financially because of Cagney's standard superior performance and an outstanding supporting cast headed by Mae Clarke.

Another noteworthy event of 1936 for Cagney was the realization of a longstanding dream — the purchase of a farm on Martha's Vineyard. "I can't think of anything more satisfactory, more life fulfilling, than living on a farm surrounded by salt water," he later stated. "I used to lie in my California bed and dream of that old house in its very happy state of quiet decay. I loved it beyond words."

Cagney made a second Grand National picture during the time his Warner Bros. contract was in litigation. *Something to Sing About* (1937) was not only his first musical since *Footlight Parade* (1933), but was also a blatant expression of Cagney's (and Grand National's) view of the Hollywood industry. It is the story of Terry Rooney (Cagney), a shy bandleader who becomes a movie star in spite of the efforts of a deceitful studio boss (Gene Lockhart) to prevent it. The film received poor reviews and was shunned by audiences, however, it did contain several excellent dance sequences and was "a particular pleasure for me to do because it meant working with Harland Dixon and Johnny Boyle, two great dancers I had admired for years in vaudeville."

The courts ruled, in late 1937, that Cagney had been wrongfully worked beyond the limitations of his contract and ordered Warner Bros. to make restitution. Warners responded by guaranteeing him at least $150,000 per picture and also promised that no more than two Cagney films would be released each year. They also hired William Cagney as an associate producer.

During his stint with Grand National, Cagney had dropped off the "top ten box-office personalities" list. This fact was no doubt due to the problems faced, even today, by most non-major studios — lack of promotional funds and distribu-

With Pat O'Brien in *The Fighting 69th* (1940).

tion strength. When Cagney was reconciled with Warner Bros., Grand National lost its big box-office draw and was forced to cancel future productions. One of the pictures they cancelled was *Angels with Dirty Faces,* which reverted to its writer, who then sold it to Warners. It became one of the two films that Cagney appeared in in 1938.

Boy Meets Girl (1938) was Cagney's first film of that year. He co-starred with Pat O'Brien in this satire about Hollywood in which two screen writers create a scheme to make a movie star out of an infant. Frank McHugh, Marie Wilson, and Ralph Bellamy made strong appearances that lent gusto to the otherwise weak scenario.

Angels with Dirty Faces (1938) stands out as one of Cagney's finest motion pictures. In it he co-stars with Humphrey Bogart, Ann Sheridan, Pat O'Brien, and the Dead End Kids. It's the story of gangster Rocky Sullivan (Cagney) who returns to his neighborhood after a long absence and is reunited with Jerry Connelly (O'Brien), who now is

Relaxing with Jeffrey Lynn (r.) on the set of *The Fighting 69th* (1940).

On Location for *Torrid Zone* (1940). Left to right: Ann Sheridan, Cagney, Andy Devine and Pat O'Brien.

A scene from *City for Conquest* (1941). Left to right: Ann Sheridan, Frank McHugh, Cagney, and Anthony Quinn.

the local priest, and James Frazier (Bogart), Rocky's dishonest lawyer, who is now a club owner. The priest is attempting to rid the city of criminals; the lawyer and a crooked politician (George Bancroft) plot to dispose of him. Rocky kills the duo to save the priest, but he is arrested and eventually sentenced to die. Just before Rocky goes to the electric chair, the priest pleads with him to feign cowardice so the hero image that the street gang (the Dead End Kids) has of him will be destroyed. The final scene, when Rocky falls to his knees in convulsions, was directed and

(Above) With Frank McHugh (l.) and Elia Kazan (c.) in
City for Conquest (1940).

(Below) A scene from *The Strawberry Blonde* (1941).
Left to right: Rita Hayworth, Olivia de Havilland,
Cagney, and Jack Carson.

portrayed with such subtlety that the audience
never really knows whether Rocky has died a hero
or a coward.

Angels with Dirty Faces is considered one of
the best gangster films of the late 1930s. It received glowing reviews and made a lot of money
at the box office. Cagney received the New York
Film Critics' award for Best Actor of 1938 and was
also nominated for his first Oscar as Best Actor.

Rocky Sullivan is the Cagney role most often
imitated by impressionists, and while the enter-
tainers may succeed in reminding us of Cagney,
they are inaccurate in their representation of the
character. "Rocky was in part modeled on a fella I
used to see when I was a kid. He was a hophead
and a pimp with four gals in his string. He worked
out of a Hungarian rathskellar on First Avenue
and 77th Street. All day long he would stand on

With Bette Davis in *The Bride Came C.O.D.* (1941).

that corner, hitch up his trousers, twist his neck, move his necktie, lift his shoulders, snap his fingers, then bring his hands together in a soft smack. The Cagney mimics I've seen don't hitch the trousers so much as just put their hands out in front and kind of wag their heads a bit. Most of them also say 'all right you guys,' which I don't remember ever saying. Moreover, I never said 'you dirty rat.' "

Co-star Humphrey Bogart said of Cagney in *The Oklahoma Kid* (1939): "He looked like a mushroom under a huge Western hat." Playing in his first Western, Cagney, as Jim Kincaid, chases the murderers of his father, brings them back either dead or alive, and rides into the sunset with the leading lady (Rosemary Lane). Bogart plays Whip McCord, one of the scoundrels who lynched Kincaid's father. *The New York Times* observed:

Clowning on location in Death Valley for *The Bride Came C.O.D.* (1941).

"There's something entirely disarming about the way [Cagney] tackled horse opera, not pretending a minute to be anything but New York's Jimmy Cagney all dressed up for a dude ranch."

In *Each Dawn I Die* (1939), Cagney plays Frank Ross, a journalist who is framed by a crooked district attorney on a manslaughter charge and sent to prison. On the inside, Ross is befriended by Hood Stacy (George Raft), a notorious gangster.

This film about prison life climaxes with a bloody prisoner uprising in which Stacy is killed. Ross survives, however, and labors to reform prison conditions. The New York *Daily Mirror* remarked: "Raft and Cagney never have been better."

The Roaring Twenties (1939) stars Cagney as Eddie Bartlett, a cabdriver turned bootlegger. Humphrey Bogart plays George Hally, a cruel gangster and fellow bootlegger. Lloyd Hart (Jef-

(Above and right) Publicity photographs, early 1940's.

Practicing dance routines with sister Jeanne Cagney for *Yankee Doodle Dandy* (1942).

frey Lynn) is a lawyer and the husband of Jean (Priscilla Lane) whom Bartlett loves. Frank McHugh plays Bartlett's pal. In the story, Bartlett and Hally are successful rum runners, but they eventually become rivals and their gang splits apart. With the end of Prohibition and the start of the Depression, Bartlett loses everything except one taxicab. Years later, Jean hires what turns out to be Bartlett's cab. She informs him that Hally,

still dishonest and wealthy, plans to murder her husband, who is now the assistant district attorney. Bartlett agrees to see Hally and try to convince him to change his mind. There is a series of shoot-outs and both Hally and Bartlett die.

Because of the force of Cagney and Bogart's acting, the film is thought of by many to be a minor masterpiece, as well as symbolic of the end of traditional gangster movies. Asked about the

With S. Z. Sakall (c.) and Richard Whorf (r.) in *Yankee Doodle Dandy* (1942).

artistic merits of scripts such as *The Roaring Twenties,* Cagney replied: "Writers were pressed to crank out their stuff by the yard, and consequently there was a limited story line in all their things. An example of this was the first day of shooting *The Roaring Twenties.* Our director, Raoul Walsh,

asked me how I liked the opening scene as written, and I said I thought it was pretty bad, as indeed it was. Frank McHugh had a replacement in mind, and we decided to go with it. Those pictures were sheer product, and if anyone was practicing art, I never saw it. While we were on the set of *The Roar-*

As George M. Cohen in *Yankee Doodle Dandy* (1942).

A lightfooted scene from *Yankee Doodle Dandy* (1942).

ing Twenties, we made changes constantly, hoping to bring life to the silly thing."

Cagney declared on more than one occasion that the Hollywood ambiance and social scene in no way appealed to him. His associates found him to be a friendly, private man who fancied hosting storytelling, joke-sharing evenings with a few friends; large parties and gatherings of strangers made him feel uncomfortable and out of place. "By the late 1930s, my pattern of living was fairly well set. Learn the words, do the scenes, and then when the picture was finished, without any delay,

Publicity photograph, 1942.

(Right) On the train to Mexico, with Joan Blondell, 1942.

Cagney receives a hug and kiss from his wife after winning an Oscar for *Yankee Doodle Dandy* (1942).

With Van Heflin (l.), Greer Garson (c.) and Teresa Wright (r.), at the Academy Awards, 1943. Heflin and Wright earned Oscars for Best Supporting Actor and Actress; Garson earned an Oscar for Best Actress.

back East to Martha's Vineyard."

By 1940, James Cagney was one of the highest paid individuals in America. (In 1939 alone, he paid over $100,000 in taxes.) Part of his income was derived from radio performances: the Lux Radio Theatre, the Gertrude Lawrence Revlon Review, and others. In 1940, Cagney performed in the radio adaptation of Dalton Trumbo's searing work, *Johnny Got His Gun,* about which Cagney

stated: "I did it for nothing because it was a brilliant argument against war." (Actually, he was forced to accept a minimum fee because of a ruling by the new Radio Actors Guild.)

William Keighly directed Cagney in two 1940 releases: *The Fighting 69th* and *Torrid Zone. The Fighting 69th* is based on the exploits of a famous World War I Irish regiment from New York. "What with all the Micks in the stock company, it did

Publicity photograph.

(Left) Publicity photograph, 1940s.

seem a natural," said Cagney. Pat O'Brien, Frank McHugh, Alan Hale, George Brent, and Tommy Dugan co-starred in this story of a soldier's (Cagney) initial insubordination, cowardice, and eventual battlefield heroics. The film's script was hastily thrown together, but its acting, superb photography, and publicity budget made the film a box-office success. It was the only film in which Cagney appeared with an all-male cast.

Torrid Zone (1940) was the eighth and last movie in which Cagney and Pat O'Brien appeared together. Cagney plays a gun-slinging troubleshooter in South America; O'Brien plays the white-suited owner of a nearby banana plantation. Both men vie for the affections of Ann Sheridan. The movie was criticized for being a silly comedy of little redeeming value.

In 1941, Cagney starred in *City for Conquest,* which also featured Ann Sheridan, Anthony Quinn, Frank Craven, Donald Crisp, and Elia Kazan (acting, not directing). Cagney plays Danny Kenny, a truck driver who becomes a professional boxer and is then blinded when one of his opponents rubs a toxic substance into his eyes. "I worked like a dog on *City for Conquest.* When I saw the final cut of the picture, it was quite a surprise. The studio had edited out the best scenes, excellent stuff, leaving only a skeleton of the original work. What remained was a trite melodrama. That cured me of seeing my films thenceforth. I even wrote a letter of apology to the author. Yet *City for Conquest* did well at the box office, which ought to prove something or other."

In December of 1940, the Cagneys adopted their first child, three-year-old James, Jr.; soon after, they adopted their daughter Cathleen (called Casey).

The Strawberry Blonde (1941) was adapted from James Hagen's Broadway play *One Sunday Afternoon.* It was the second, and considered the best, of three film versions of that play. The story takes place in lower Manhattan at the turn of the century. Rita Hayworth plays Virginia, the strawberry blonde Biff Grimes (Cagney) falls in love with. But, Virginia elopes with wealthy Hugo Barnstead (Jack Carson), and Biff later marries Amy Lind (Olivia de Havilland). Some years later,

Hugo offers Biff a vice-presidency in his contracting firm, and Biff accepts. When Biff is falsely convicted of negligence, he is sent to prison, where he earns a diploma in dentistry. Soon after his release, he receives a call from Hugo, who needs a tooth pulled. Instead of killing Hugo, which was his original plan for revenge, Biff decides to perform the operation without using any anesthesia. "After all," says Biff, "I'm a happy man and he is not." *The Strawberry Blonde* had a superb cast and script; the comedy was well received by critics and fans alike.

The Bride Came C.O.D. (1941) was also a comedy and starred Cagney as airplane pilot Steve Collins who is commissioned to return an oil tycoon's daughter (Bette Davis) to her home in Amarillo, Texas, but crashes in the desert in the process. "I've never seen that one," said Cagney, "but I have no reason to doubt Bette's word when she wrote in her autobiography: 'We both reached bottom with this one.'"

By the end of 1941, Cagney was 42 years old and, as such, was too old for combat duty during World War II, but this did little to quell his enthusiasm for becoming involved in the war effort; he applied his talents to special fund-raising projects such as the March of Dimes and The Motion Picture Relief Fund; he became chairman of the Hollywood Victory Committee, which went on war bond selling tours; he gave his yacht to the U.S. Coast Guard to use for training; and he turned over his beloved summer estate on Martha's Vineyard to the U.S. Army to use for maneuvers. He traveled with the Hollywood Victory Caravan, a bond-selling, troup-entertaining tour composed of Hollywood performers. He also traveled overseas to entertain troops and appeared in numerous recruiting and training films for all the branches of the armed services.

Perhaps the only distinctive quality of *Captains of the Clouds* (1942) is that it marked Cagney's first appearance in Technicolor. He plays Brian MacLean, a cocky American bush pilot who joins the Royal Canadian Air Force just prior to World War II. Michael Curtiz directed, and there are some stunning aerial sequences, but the project as a whole was regarded as uninspired by the critics.

On a tour of American military units in Europe, 1944, Cagney signs a British fan's autograph book.

After two successive film flops, Cagney needed a superior project to regain some of his faltering professional esteem. It was also at this time that song and dance man George M. Cohan was looking for the right studio and the right actor to film his life story. He chose Warner Bros. and James Cagney, and *Yankee Doodle Dandy* (1942) was born.

Yankee Doodle Dandy is the story of George M.'s beginnings in vaudeville, his Broadway successes, and his retirement years. Cagney's sister Jeanne co-stars as Cohan's sister, Walter Huston and Rosemary DeCamp play his parents, and Michael Curtiz directed this fast-paced musical extravaganza. The film was a homecoming for Cagney—the chance to sing and dance in what many considered the ultimate part. "The answer to the question, Which of my films is my favorite? is simple. It

derives from George M. Cohan's comment about himself: 'Once a song and dance man, always a song and dance man.' In that brief statement, you have my life story; those few words tell as much about me professionally as there is to tell."

This patriotic movie, full of show-stopping company numbers, skilled dancing, easy moving dialogue, and tender moments won over all its viewers, including an ailing George M. Cohan. He sent Cagney a telegram of thanks and approval: "So *Yankee Doodle Dandy* turned out to be something I could take real pride in."

The film was nominated for eight Academy Awards. It won three—including Best Actor for James Cagney. It was the only Oscar he ever received.

Yankee Doodle Dandy not only contributed an important nationalistic spirit to the war effort, it contributed quite a bit of money as well. All box-office receipts from the New York, Los Angeles, and London premieres were given to the war treasury. The amount of these proceeds was considerable. For example, in New York the ticket prices for opening night ranged from $25,000 for each of the "best" seats to $25 for the "worst." On that one night, the receipts totaled $5,750,000 and ultimately purchased three Liberty cargo vessels for the Atlantic Convoy.

After completing *Yankee Doodle Dandy*, Cagney, who was now president of the Screen Actors Guild, again approached Warner Bros. with a demand to re-negotiate his contract. Warners refused to negotiate, and Cagney discovered that they had doctored their accounting ledgers to slight his income from box-office receipts. "So that marked the end of that. I walked out again, and brother Bill and I formed a little company to make our own pictures."

The first effort of William Cagney Productions was *Johnny Come Lately* (1943) for United Artists. In this nostalgic piece, Cagney plays Tom Richards, a vagabond with a good heart who, along with a small town newspaper publisher (Grace George), fights to expose political corruption. Although the film's plot is not engaging, it does feature a superb cast of supporting players: Hattie McDaniel, Marjorie Main, and Miss George. But, as Cagney's follow-up to *Yankee*

Entertaining returning war veterans in Los Angeles harbor. 1945.

(Right) Practicing the Martial Arts for his role in *Blood on the Sun* (1945).

Doodle Dandy, Johnny Come Lately did little to excite the critics.

The failure of Cagney's next film, *Blood on the Sun* (1945), nearly crippled William Cagney Productions for good. In this story, set in Tokyo in the 1920s, Cagney plays American newspaper editor Nick Condon who stumbles onto a secret Japanese plot that would lead them to world domination. Enraged also by their brutal murder

of two of his colleagues, he embarks on a one-man crusade to sabotage the plot. Although *Blood on the Sun,* which co-starred Sylvia Sidney, received many favorable reviews, it was a failure at the box-office.

After suffering two screen failures under his own production banner, Cagney agreed to star for Twentieth Century-Fox in *13 Rue Madeleine* (1946). In this excellent World War II espionage thriller,

The Redbook Party, Beverly Club, 1945, with Joseph Cotten (c.).

George Burns (l.) and Cagney at the 15th Anniversary Party for the Burns and Allen radio show at Hollywood's Brown Derby restaurant.

co-starring Richard Conte and Sam Jaffe, Cagney plays Bob Sharkey, the leader of a small band of O.S.S. officers who must flush out a Nazi spy in his ranks and successfully locate a German rocket launching site. Cagney worked for eight weeks and earned a salary of $300,000 in this documen-tary-style drama. The film became an immediate favorite of Cagney fans everywhere, but Cagney cared very little about that; his goal was to raise enough money to finance another Cagney Productions project.

In 1946, the Cagney brothers successfully

On location for *13 Rue Madeleine* (1946). Center left to right: Frank Lattimore, Cagney, Richard Conte, and Annabella.

(Right) With columnist Sidney Skolsky, 1947.

With playwright William Saroyan, author of the Pulitzer Prize winning drama "The Time of Your Life." Cagney starred in the movie version, in 1948.

negotiated an option on the screen adaptation of William Saroyan's prize-winning play *The Time of Your Life* (1948). It is the story of a collection of eccentric people in a San Francisco waterfront bar who spend all their time talking about their dreams. William Bendix is the bartender/owner, Wayne Morris is his pal; Jeanne Cagney plays an ex-prostitute, and James Barton, a tall-tale spinner. Cagney plays Joe, the champagne-drinking

philosopher, and Broderick Crawford and Ward Bond make brief appearances.

William Saroyan wrote Cagney: "I stood in line at the United Artists Theatre and bought a ticket to the first showing of *The Time of Your Life* in San Francisco...It wasn't more than three minutes into the film until I had forgotten that I had written the play. I was too busy enjoying it to care who wrote it...I send you congratulations,

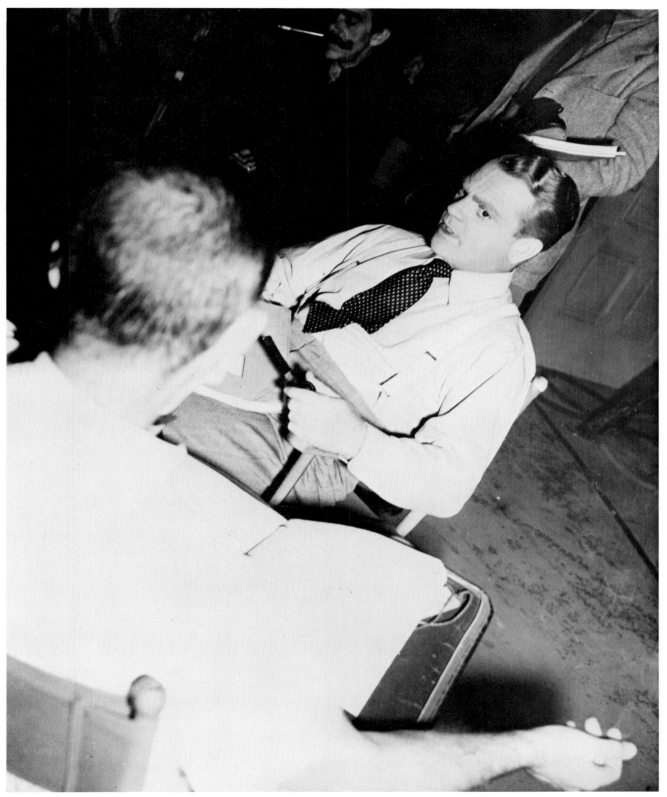

The Cagney eye holds director H.C. Potter hypnotically on the set of *The Time of Your Life* (1948).

profound thanks and all good wishes."

Few critics disliked the film, but despite the accolades, the public did not become enthusiastic about the picture. As a result, it did very poorly at the box office and left Cagney in a precarious financial position. When Warner Bros. approached him with another standard gangster script, he would have liked to have turned it down, but he needed the income to keep his production company alive. White Heat (1949), however, turned out to be one of Cagney's finest films.

Cagney plays the deranged Cody Jarrett, the leader of a gang of train robbers and hijackers. It is the first role in which the character he portrays has no redeeming traits. "The original script was very formula. The leading character was just another murderous thug. For some kind of variant, I said to the writers, 'Let's fashion this

With Edmond O'Brien (l.) between scenes of White Heat (1949).

after Ma Barker and her boys and make Cody a psychotic to account for his actions.'" Writers Ivan Goff and Ben Roberts effected changes, and what emerged was a totally despicable but memorable character.

White Heat co-starred Virginia Mayo, Margaret Wycherly, Steve Cochran, and Edmond O'Brien; it received superb notices and was viewed as a good film made better by Cagney's portrayal of the vicious, mother-fixated killer. White Heat is now considered the last of the great old-time gangster movies.

One of the few pictures Cagney will sometimes watch on television is a musical called The West Point Story (1950). Directed by Roy Del Ruth, this film was intended to approach, if not duplicate, the success of Yankee Doodle Dandy; it fell far short of that. Cagney plays a Broadway musical director who agrees to coordinate the annual West Point cadet variety show. Elwin Bixby (Cagney) discovers the talents of Tom Fletcher (Gordon MacRae), who, he believes, could be a show biz smash if he'd resign from the Academy. Virginia Mayo plays Cagney's girlfriend, and Alan Hale, Jr., and Doris Day also co-star. Cagney's energy is up to his usual high standard, and he goes through several dance numbers like a hoofer half his age (He was 51 at the time).

Bosley Crowther of The New York Times, who was one of many disappointed critics, wrote: "The measure of Mr. Cagney's impact upon the whole tenuous show is indicated when he is not on the screen. For then the thing sags in woeful fashion, the romance becomes absurd, and the patriotic chest-thumping becomes so much chorus-boy parade." Cagney's impression differed from the critics: "In West Point Story, beautiful Virginia Mayo and I did a number that I thought was some of the best dancing we ever did. [The film is] still a pleasure to look at because it showed some versatility and humor, things I prize highly and always strive for."

Cagney's next project was Kiss Tomorrow Goodbye (1950), a William Cagney Productions film, made in association with Warner Bros. Based on Horace McCoy's novel of the same name, the story concerns Ralph Cotter, a vicious gangster who tricks two crooked big city policemen into

Cagney's brother William (left), their mother, and sister Jeanne, 1948.

On his farm, with daughter Casey, 1949.

With Casey and son James, Jr. (r.) 1950.

On location for *The West Point Story* (1950), with Co-star Virginia Mayo and director Roy Del Ruth (r.).

(Right) Getting a crew cut for *The West Point Story* (1950).

becoming his pawns. This movie was produced with making money in mind; it was the first Cagney Productions film to feature continuous violence (It was so violent it was banned in Ohio), but it also presented the vileness of its characters in a totally unsympathetic way, which is how Cagney wanted it. Unfortunately, the commercial and artistic aspects were not well coordinated,

and the result was a conventional film with only hints of exceptional style or method.

Kiss Tomorrow Goodbye was directed by Gordon Douglas, and filming was rushed through in only 28 days. Barbara Payton, Ward Bond, Matt McHugh (Frank's brother), and William Frawley co-starred.

Come Fill the Cup (1951), also directed by

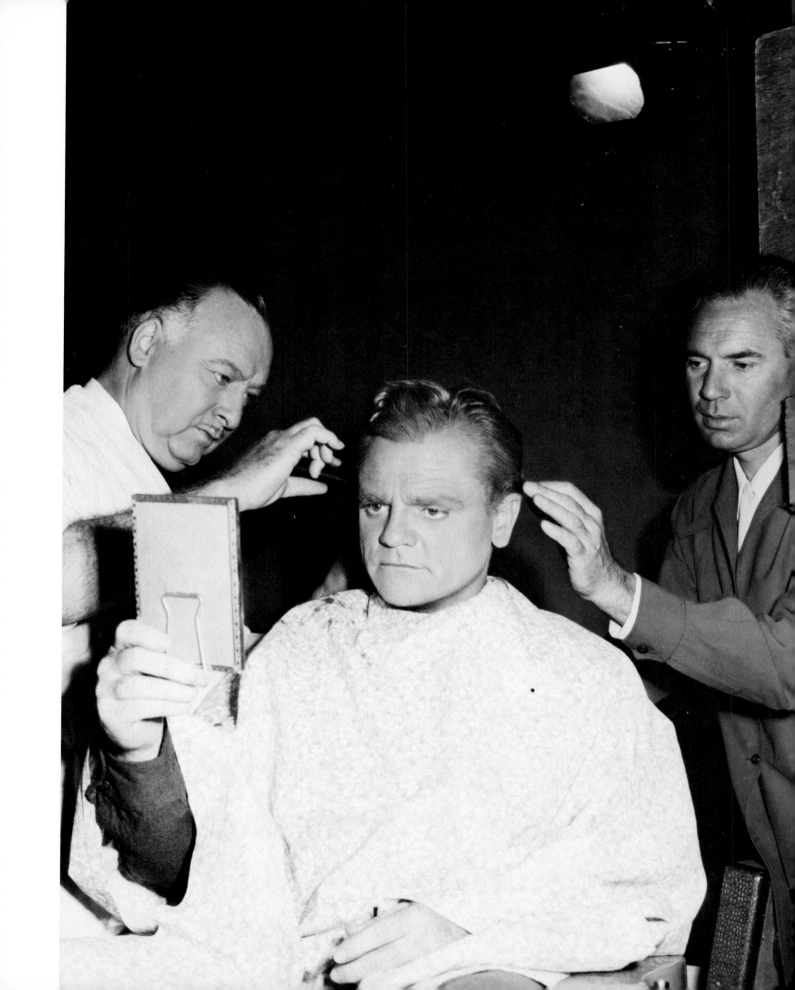

Cagney explains how he injured his left hand, 1950.
Buddy, one of his dogs, rests in his arms.

based on the actual "Operation Starlift" that transported film stars to Travis Air Force Base near San Francisco to entertain soldiers during the Korean War. Cagney appears briefly as himself. This film was a major disaster. Said *Time* magazine: "*Starlift* is guilty of its worst breach of good taste when it takes a low bow for Hollywood's patriotic gesture, makes the project seem exclusively Warners', and includes in its cast some stars who never troubled to fly up to Travis Air Base. And the $1,000,000 *Starlift* is entertaining U.S. theaters just a month after Hollywood's Operation Starlift shut down, after running out of the $5,000 that Hollywood chipped in for its expenses."

Cagney next appeared in the screen adaptation of *What Price Glory?* (1952), the Maxwell Anderson-Laurence Stallings World War I pacifist play about two soldiers (Dan Dailey and Cagney) charged with leading a company of old men and young boys into battle. "The story never struck me as being anything up my street until I heard it was going to be made as a musical. I warmed to that idea immediately and decided to take it on." Just before shooting was to begin, plans for the music were abandoned. "I was committed at that point, and I did it, but not, in Shakespeare's phrase, 'for my ease.' " Cagney plodded with Dailey through the unfunny, aimless script, and the *New York World-Telegram and Sun* wrote: "Cagney and Dailey have lowered their acting standards in keeping with the new spirit of the vehicle. The total result is deplorable, which is shocking when you see the name of John Ford as director."

A Lion in the Streets (1953), the final William Cagney Productions film, is the story of the rise to power by a backwoods Southern politician. This was truly a Cagney family project. James starred as Hank Martin, the political opportunist, Jeanne played the woman who ultimately guns the power-hungry politician down, William produced the film, and Edward edited the script. Barbara Hale and Anne Francis appeared as Martin's wife and mistress, respectively, and Raoul Walsh directed. The picture received mixed reviews and was also plagued by its similarity to the Academy Award-winning *All the King's Men* (1949) which of-

Gordon Douglas, is the story of Lew Marsh (Cagney), a crime-busting newspaper editor, and his efforts to overcome his alcoholism. Raymond Massey plays the publisher, Gig Young plays the publisher's nephew, James Gleason is Marsh's buddy, and Sheldon Leonard appears as the thug that Marsh eventually brings to justice. *Come Fill the Cup* was little more than a sob story about the pitfalls of alcoholism, but it brought the talents of a fine young actor, Gig Young, to the public's attention.

Starlift (1951) was a star-studded musical

As Hank Martin in *A Lion in the Streets* (1953).

fered a similar story line but with far greater dramatic power and artistic excellence.

Run for Cover (1955) was Cagney's first Western since *The Oklahoma Kid* (1939). It is the story of Matt Dow (Cagney), an ex-con who was wrongfully imprisoned, who travels west and becomes the sheriff of a small town. He also meets and befriends Davey Bishop (John Derek); he falls in love with Helga Swenson (Viveca Lindfors); and he becomes enmeshed in a heated conflict between a notorious gang and a band of Indians. "We had tried to make as offbeat a

With Doris Day between scenes of *Love Me or Leave Me* (1955).

Western as possible, but whoever cut the film was evidently revolted by anything but cliches. As a consequence, little things that the director and the actors put in to give the story extra dimension were excised very proficiently. The result was just another programmer." Many critics agreed.

Love Me or Leave Me (1955) is the musical biography of singer Ruth Etting, played by Doris Day. It focuses on her 17-year relationship with Martin "The Gimp" Snyder, the clubfooted gangster who sponsors Etting's career and strong-arms her into a loveless marriage. Cagney's appearance as Snyder was also his first appearance in Cinema-Scope. The screenplay was written by Daniel Fuchs and Isobel Lennart and, according to Cagney, was "the perfect script. There was nothing to be added, nothing to be taken away. I was so pleased to find one that didn't need any help, any devices." The film was an immediate hit and was nominated for six Academy Awards, including one for Cagney as Best Actor.

In 1954, John Ford called Cagney and said, in effect, How about a nice vacation? *Mister Roberts* (1955) was in the planning stages, and Ford wanted Cagney to co-star with Henry Fonda, Jack Lemmon, and William Powell in the film version of the best-selling novel and hit Broadway play of the late 1940s. The comedy-drama takes place aboard a Navy cargo vessel; Cagney is the petty tyrannical captain who makes life miserable for his crew. "I did it for a lark. It was one of the easiest pictures I ever made."

Cagney has always said that, second to song and dance movies, his favorite genre is the *Mister Roberts* type of film, a serious story with humorous overtones. The picture was nominated for three Oscars, one of which was won by Jack Lemmon for Best Supporting Actor for his role as Ensign Pulver.

Not long after *Mister Roberts* was released, Cagney, Fonda, Lemmon, and others from the film appeared in a brief scene from the movie on "The Ed Sullivan Show" on CBS-Television.

The Seven Little Foys (1955) starred Bob Hope as the vaudeville song and dance man Eddie Foy, and Cagney appeared briefly in the movie as George M. Cohan. "Hope's invitation to do George M. coincided neatly with my desire to lose

As the captain in *Mister Roberts* (1955).

fifteen pounds. So he and I rehearsed the dance for three weeks and I lost my unwanted lard."

1955 was also an important year in Cagney's personal life. In that year, he seriously began painting; he began to spend more time with an old passion, writing poetry; and he and Bill left their farm on Martha's Vineyard and moved to Duchess County, New York.

"When I bought the New York farm, I grew even closer to the country. Outside of my family, the prime concern of my life has been nature and its order, and how we have savagely been altering

With Henry Fonda (r.) in *Mister Roberts* (1955).

As the captain in *Mister Roberts* (1955).

(Right) Cagney loads hay in the barn while his wife Bill looks on, 1955.

that order." Cagney is a bitter opponent of all polluters and pillagers of the land, and in 1955, he began to make occasional appearances at local colleges to lecture on land conservation.

He also began to contact the people he believed to be the enemies of conservation. And he did so in a very personal way. To his foes in the highway construction business, Cagney wrote:

Lay down the ribbon of concrete, boys
And we'll divvy up lots of loot;
We do it all quiet and neat, boys,
At ten thousand dollars a foot.
We'll certainly take care of our friends, boys
As we give the law the bend, boys...

And to the strip miners:

Tear the tops off the mountains
And terrace the slopes,
For the land must be ready
For dingbats and dopes.

("And if that sound bitter, let me say I mean it to be bitter.")

Tribute to a Bad Man (1956) was an MGM Western about an aging horse rancher in the Colorado Rockies who takes the law into his own hands to stop the rustling of his stock. Cagney plays Jeremy Rodock, the rancher; Don Dubbins is Steve Miller, Rodock's hired hand; and Irene

On the Farm, 1950s.

James Stewart (l.) and Orson Welles (r.) extend best wishes to Cagney as filming, begins for *Man of a Thousand Faces* (1957).

Getting set for a scene in *Man of a Thousand Faces* (1957). Cagney is dressed as a clown (r.).

Papas makes her American film debut as Jocasta, Rodock's mistress.

The Rodock character was another tough guy with likable qualities—a type of personality few actors have portrayed more powerfully than Cagney. "Any way you look at it," said *The New York Times,* "the old master James Cagney really is at home in *Tribute to a Bad Man*...The eyes narrow, the nose wrinkles, the mouth twists arrogant-ly, the forefinger coolly grips the trigger and the voice, oozing venom, says 'Do-o-on't move.' And nobody moves."

These Wilder Years (1956) is the story of Steve Bradford (Cagney), a wealthy, lonely, middle-aged man in search of the illegitimate son he fathered years earlier. The screenplay primarily involves the bitter rivalry between Bradford and Ann Dempster (Barbara Stanwyck), the head of the

Getting into the mood for his role as a New York waterfront boss in *Never Steal Anything Small* (1958).

adoption agency that had placed his child twenty years before. Don Dubbins plays Bradford's son Mark; Walter Pidgeon is a lawyer; and Betty Lou Keim is Suzie, the young unwed mother whom Bradford befriends and eventually adopts. *These Wilder Years* was neither a critical nor a financial success.

1956 was also a year of departures from the motion picture screen for Cagney. On May 24th,

he acted as master of ceremonies at the White House Correspondents' Association dinner at which President Eisenhower was in attendance. In recognition of Cagney's continuing generosity to and involvement with many relief drives, the president offered this brief tribute: "No one in show business has a warmer heart or has done more for the less privileged."

On September 10, 1956, Cagney appeared

live on NBC-Television as Army Sergeant George Bridgeman in Robert Wallace's *Soldier from the Wars Returning* on "Robert Montgomery Presents." This play, which was specially written for Cagney, follows the cynical sergeant as he escorts home the body of a soldier killed in the Korean War. Cagney received excellent reviews, but the play as a whole did not. Cagney claims he appeared in it only as a favor to his good friend Montgomery. "I've had no real interest in television at any time. I simply couldn't work up any kind of enthusiasm for it."

Cagney's next film role, *Man of a Thousand Faces* (1957), was a major success for him. His rendering of the troubled and talented Lon Chaney, Sr., was one of his most memorable performances. But although the film was filled with scenes of masterful acting by Cagney: he pantomimes, re-creates Chaney's hunchback Quasimodo, and dons numerous personages as expertly as the real Chaney did, it was not the smash hit it might have been. Some critics concluded that even Cagney's virtuoso performance did not make up for the inherent weaknesses of its script, and they branded *Man of a Thousand Faces* as overly melodramatic.

Others felt, however that the movie was one of the best biographies about a Hollywood personality ever filmed and that Cagney's portrayal of Chaney favorably compared with his portrayal of George M. Cohan in *Yankee Doodle Dandy*.

"A.C. Lyles, an old friend, came to me in 1957 and asked me to direct his Paramount production of *Short Cut to Hell* (1957). I was moved to do it out of friendship only. I did it for nothing [minimum salary plus a percentage of the profits], and in just twenty days, which was long enough for me. Directing I find a bore; I have no interest in telling other people their business." *Short Cut to Hell* was a low budget remake of *This Gun for Hire*. Robert Ivers stars as Kyle, a professional killer in search of a man who is cheating him; Georgann Johnson appears as his girlfriend, Glory. Some critics praised the film, others did not, but at the very least, the picture was considered newsworthy because it was Cagney's first directing job. It was also his last.

The story of the musical comedy-drama *Never Steal Anything Small* (1958) is explained by

Celebrating his 30th year as an actor, Cagney offers Mae Clarke a grapefruit, as they recall a famous scene in *The Public Enemy* (1931).

an announcement that precedes the film's opening scene: "This picture is sympathetically dedicated to labor and its problems in coping with a new and merry type of public enemy...the charming, well-dressed gentleman who cons his way to a union throne and never needs to blow a safe again." Cagney plays Jake McIllaney, a hoodlum stevedore who steals from company coffers and arranges for his election as president of the United Stevedore Workers' Union. Shirley Jones co-stars along with Roger Smith and Cara Williams. The picture was Cagney's fifth and final song and dance movie. The music, by Allie Wrubel and Maxwell Anderson, received terrible notices, as did the picture as a whole. Cagney's

On location in Ireland for *Shake Hands with the Devil* (1959). Actress Glynis Johns braves the cold wind and water in a bathing suit.

Dancing to keep fit while filming *Shake Hands with the Devil* (1959). His accompanist, Miss Julia Grey of Dublin, Ireland, runs a fish market when not playing for Cagney.

(Left) Sharing a joke with actress Dana Wynter on location for *Shake Hands with the Devil* (1959).

presence in it was seen as its sole redeeming value.

One of Cagney's favorite films was shot in Ireland. It is *Shake Hand with the Devil* (1959) in which he plays Sean Lenihan, an Irish surgeon who joins the revolutionary underground during the struggle for Irish "home rule" in 1921. Lenihan is a

fanatic—more so than his comrades in the Irish Republican Army. The doctor becomes obsessed with his dream of Irish independence and at one point prepares to kill a member of the royal family. Don Murray, playing Lenihan's friend, an American visiting Ireland, shoots Lenihan when it

At a press conference in New York, with retired Fleet Admiral William F. Halsey, after it was announced that Cagney would portray Halsey in *The Gallant Hours* (1960).

Between scenes during filming of *The Gallant Hours* (1960). Cagney checks the equipment of Robert Montgomery, Jr (l.), while co-star Robert Montgomery checks the equipment of Cagney's son James, Jr.

becomes apparent that the surgeon has lost all sense of rational behavior. The film's theme is a familiar one for Cagney: violence corrupts. Indeed, the title is derived from the Irish proverb, "Those who shake hands with the devil often have trouble getting their hands back."

Cagney made the picture hoping he could add the element of virtuous principle to his standard violence-loving stereotype. "During my career, thousands of words have been written about me. Most of them dwelt on the fact that I am, by vocation, a farmer; that off screen I lead a quiet life and don't get into trouble. But none of these stories has anywhere near the impact of one of my pictures. People get an impression of me from the screen that sticks much more thoroughly than anything they read." Sean Lenihan is murderous, but he has a cause beyond his own aggressiveness. Cagney had always wanted to portray this type of character, and to be able to do so on location in the lush Irish countryside gave him even more joy.

Although he was born a New York Irishman, everywhere Cagney traveled in Ireland while working on *Shake Hands with the Devil,* he was hailed as the local boy who made good. Cagney, in turn, became involved with the people and the problems of his ancestral country. When he learned of the Irish government's plan to mine and industrialize much of the green hills he had come to love, he wrote the Irish *Times*:

> You want to see Shannon like the Hudson?
> Or the Liffey just as filthy as the Seine?
> Bring in the arrogant asses
> And their garbage and their gasses
> The pollutants plunging poison down each
>   drain:
> Killing everything that's living
> For which nature's unforgiving,
> And the punishment will certainly fit the
>   crime.
> Where man, the creeping cancer,
> Will have to make the final answer
> As he smothers 'neath his self-created
>   slime.

Upon completing *Shake Hands with the*

Discussing a scene for *The Gallant Hours* (1960) with actor Robert Montgomery (r.). Montgomery produced and directed the film.

Taking a breather during the filming of *The Gallant Hours* (1960).

Devil, Cagney considered permanently retiring to his farm in New York. But in 1960, he agreed again to work for his friend Robert Montgomery and appear as Admiral William "Bull" Halsey in *The Gallant Hours* (1960).

Working on this film was a labor of love for Cagney, who was a long-time admirer of the Admiral. Montgomery directed this war story which focused on the inner turmoil of a commander on the spot. The film covers a five-week period in 1942 when American naval forces battled the Japanese in the Pacific. Dennis Weaver and Karl

Swenson co-star, and both Cagney and Montgomery's sons appear as extras. The story begins with Halsey's retirement, and his career is traced through flashbacks. Unfortunately *The Gallant Hours* was of poor overall quality and did not command significant attention.

Billy Wilder persuaded Cagney to make *One, Two, Three* (1961) by delivering a script that warned that a rapid-fire pace was required of Cagney should he decide to accept the part of C. P. MacNamara. MacNamara is an aggressive Coca-Cola executive in cold war West Berlin who must babysit a coddled American teenager (Pamela Tiffin), his boss's daughter. When she marries a Marxist East Berliner (Horst Buchholz), MacNamara must transform him into a suitable husband.

Cagney was fascinated by the opportunity to play a totally comedic role, and he hadn't worked in a pure comedy film since the 1930s. In June 1961, he reported for work at a studio in West Germany and stayed until September. The result was 100 minutes of nonstop one-liners, and he brought a vitality to the part of MacNamara that far exceeded the expectations of everyone involved in the project. About Cagney's performance, the *Saturday Review* said: "He shouts his way through the entire movie, bellowing and bowling over all opposition. After awhile I found myself flinching every time he gathered his breath. A man just can't keep that up without strain to the vital organs."

After the successful release of *One, Two, Three,* Cagney met with friend Charles Champlin of the *Los Angeles Times* to officially announce his retirement from the screen: "In this business you need enthusiasm. I just don't have it for acting anymore. After all, acting is not the beginning and the end of everything . . . I was always a journeyman actor; I never gave a damn about the rest of it. Do the job and run. I don't need the applause. I figured the days aren't long enough for doing all the things that are fun and interesting. Acting was always a second choice with me; I was always aiming at the farm. Not long ago I drove down Ventura Boulevard past Warner Bros. where I made over forty of my films, and I didn't turn a hair. It didn't interest me one damn. After *One, Two, Three* was completed, I didn't even bother to

Ronald Reagan (l.), Mrs. Reagan, and Cagney at a Screen Actors Guild rally, Hollywood, 1960.

see the picture and I don't think I ever will. All this for the simplest of reasons: I'm just not that much interested. I had the career. It was fine, I enjoyed it, but it [is] over."

Cagney was later offered the role of Alfred Doolittle in the screen version of *My Fair Lady,* and he was tempted to take it, but true to his word, he declined and made no other film appearances after *One, Two, Three.* He did, however, dabble in several related activities: in 1962, he narrated a CBS-Television anti-Communist documentary entitled "Road to the Wall;" in 1966, he was one of the voices in the U. S. Forestry Service animated film, *The Ballad of Smokey the Bear,* which ap-

With Arlene Francis and director Billy Wilder on the set of *One, Two, Three* (1961).

peared on television on the "General Electric Theater;" in 1968, he voiced-over an introduction to Paramount's *Arizona Bushwackers,* a "Grade B" Western that starred Yvonne DeCarlo and Howard Keel; and in 1973, he honored Edward G. Robinson in a posthumous special Academy Awards tribute — but again with a voice-over, not with a personal appearance.

In 1974, the American Film Institute chose James Cagney to receive their second annual Life Achievement Award (The first went to director John Ford). To everyone's surprise and delight,

Cagney, who's landed many a blow himself, feels the power of heavyweight champ Floyd Paterson's right.

Cagney agreed to attend the nationally televised, star-studded affair and accept the award in person. This event marked his first public appearance in thirteen years.

"You must be very proud [of your success]," a European star once said to him.

"I'm not," he replied.

"Why?"

"Because I had nothing to do with it. If whatever I had to sell was acceptable to the audience, where did it come from? You can't take bows for having blue eyes. The things I am

Publicity photograph, *One, Two, Three* (1961).

(Left) Returning from Germany, Cagney waits to clear customs in New York.

were passed on to me from someone else. It doesn't necessarily follow that the fellow who makes the big splash ever did anything on his own."

"But you exerted yourself."

"Yes, but where did that capacity for exten- sion come from? Did I generate the thing? Not all all. It was there."

James Cagney is a fortunate man. He loved and was loved by his parents and family; he mar- ried a woman who became his life-long partner;

Leaving church after the marriage of his son James, Jr., 1961.

he helped successfully raise two children; he has enjoyed the company of good friends; and by distinguishing himself in his chosen career and as a concerned citizen, he has earned the respect and admiration of millions of people around the world. Today, he revels in the retirement he planned for himself back in the 1930s when he bought his first farm. He tends cattle, paints, enjoys the fresh country air, and writes verse:

Why do you weep, poor dear old man?
It hurts me within when you weep.

I weep for the long lost wonderful years
I once thought were mine to keep.

Why would you keep them, poor dear old
*   man?*
That's too much to ask. Just living those
*   so-called*
Wonderful years is life's most onerous task.
For time passes and life passes and all
Things end in sadness,
Except for those sometimes fortunate ones
Who find peace in a benevolent madness.

At the American Film Institute dinner in his honor, 1974. It was Cagney's first public appearance in 13 years.

2 THE FILMS OF JAMES CAGNEY

(Left) With Lucille LaVerne in *Sinner's Holiday* (1930).

1930 **SINNER'S HOLIDAY** (Warner Bros.). Director, John G. Adolfi. Cast included: Joan Blondell, Evalyn Knapp, Lucille LaVerne, and Grant Withers. Screenplay, George Roesner and Harvey Thew; based on the play "Penny Arcade" by Marie Baumer.

1930 **DOORWAY TO HELL** (Warner Bros.). Director, Archie Mayo. Cast included: Lew Ayres, Leon Janney, Charles Judels, and Dorothy Matthews. Screenplay, George Roesner; adapted from a story by Rowland Brown.

With Lew Ayers (l.) and Dorothy Mathews in *The Doorway to Hell* (1930)

(Right) With George Arliss in *The Millionaire* (1931).

1931 **OTHER MEN'S WOMEN** (Warner Bros.). Director, William Wellman. Cast included: Mary Astor, Joan Blondell, Regis Toomey, and Grant Withers. Screenplay, William K. Wells; from a story by Maude Fulton.

1931 **THE MILLIONAIRE** (Warner Bros.). Director, John G. Adolfi. Cast included: George Arliss, Evalyn Knapp, and David Manners. Screenplay, Maude T. Howell and Julian Josephson; based on a novel by Earl Derr Biggers.

With Edward Woods (l.c.) in *The Public Enemy* (1931).

1931 **THE PUBLIC ENEMY** (Warner Bros.). Director, William Wellman. Cast included: Joan Blondell, Mae Clarke, Donald Cook, Jean Harlow, and Edward Woods. Screenplay, John Bright and Kubec Glasmon; from a story by Bright.

With Evalyn Knapp and Edward G. Robinson (c.) in
Smart Money (1931).

1931 **SMART MONEY** (Warner Bros.). Director, Alfred E.
Green. Cast included: Boris Karloff, Evalyn Knapp, and
Edward G. Robinson. Screenplay, John Bright and Kubec
Glasmon; taken from a story by Lucien Hubbard.

With Joan Blondell in *Blonde Crazy* (1931).

(Right) With Loretta Young in *Taxi!* (1931).

1931 **BLONDE CRAZY** (Warner Bros.). Director, Roy Del Ruth. Cast included: Joan Blondell, Louis Calhern, Noel Francis, and Guy Kibbee. Screenplay, John Bright and Kubec Glasman; adapted from a story by Glasmon.

1931 **TAXI!** (Warner Bros.). Director, Roy Del Ruth. Cast included: Guy Kibbee, George E. Stone, and Loretta Young. Screenplay, John Bright and Kubec Glasmon; based on the play "The Blind Spot" by Kenyon Nicholson.

With Ann Dvorak in *The Crowd Roars* (1932).

1932 **THE CROWD ROARS** (Warner Bros.). Director, Howard Hawks. Cast included: Joan Blondell, Ann Dvorak, Guy Kibbee, Eric Linden, and Frank McHugh. Screenplay, John Bright, Niven Busch, Kubec Glasmon, and Seton I. Miller; from a story by Howard Hawks.

126

(Left) With Virginia Bruce in *Winner Take All* (1932).

With Mary Brian in *Hard to Handle* (1933).

1932 **WINNER TAKE ALL** (Warner Bros.). Director, Roy Del Ruth. Cast included: Virginia Bruce, Guy Kibbee, Clarence Muse, and Marian Nixon. Screenplay, Robert Lord and Wilson Mizner; based on a story by Gerald Beaumont.

1933 **HARD TO HANDLE** (Warner Bros.). Director, Mervyn LeRoy. Cast included: Mary Brian, Claire Dodd, Ruth Donnelly, and Allen Jenkins. Screenplay, Robert Lord and Wilson Mizner; from a story by Houston Branch.

With Ralph Bellamy (c.) and Alice White in *Picture Snatcher* (1933).

1933 **PICTURE SNATCHER** (Warner Bros.). Director, Lloyd Bacon. Cast included: Ralph Bellamy, Patricia Ellis, and Alice White. Screenplay, Allen Rivkin and P. J. Wolfson; based on a story by Danny Ahearn.

1933 **THE MAYOR OF HELL** (Warner Bros.). Director, Archie Mayo. Cast included: Frankie Darro, Dudley Digges, Madge Evans, Farina, and Allen Jenkins, Screenplay, Edward Chodorov, from a story by Islin Auster.

With Madge Evans (c.) in *The Mayor of Hell* (1933).

As Chester Kent in *Footlight Parade* (1933).

1933 **FOOTLIGHT PARADE** (Warner Bros.). Director, Lloyd Bacon. Cast included: Joan Blondell, Claire Dodd, Ruth Donnelly. Hugh Herbert, Ruby Keeler, Guy Kibbee, Frank McHugh, and Dick Powell. Screenplay, Manuel Seff and James Seymour.

(Above) With Mae Clarke in *Lady Killer* (1933).

(Left) With James Eagle (l.) and George Chandler (r.) in *He Was Her Man* (1934).

1933 **LADY KILLER** (Warner Bros.). Director, Roy Del Ruth. Cast included: Mae Clarke, Leslie Fenton, and Margaret Lindsay. Screenplay, Lillie Hayward and Ben Markson; adapted from a story by Rosalind Keating Shaffer.

1934 **JIMMY THE GENT** (Warner Bros.). Director, Michael Curtiz. Cast included: Bette Davis, Alan Dinehart, Arthur Hohl, Allen Jenkins, and Alice White. Screenplay, Bertram Milhauser; based on a story by Laird Doyle and Ray Nazarro.

(Above) With Bette Davis in *Jimmy the Gent* (1934).

(Right) With Frank McHugh (c.l.), Gloria Stuart (c.) and Pat O'Brien (c.r.) in *Here Comes the Navy* (1934).

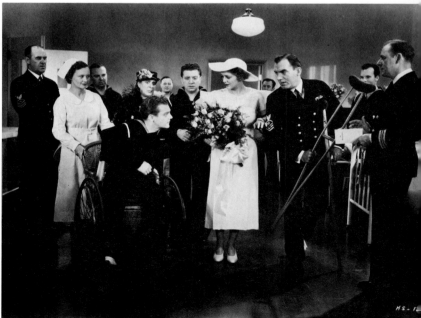

1934 HE WAS HER MAN (Warner Bros.). Director, Lloyd Bacon. Cast included: Joan Blondell, Frank Craven, Harold Huber, and Victor Jory. Screenplay, Tom Buckingham and Niven Busch; taken from a story by Robert Lord.

1934 HERE COMES THE NAVY (Warner Bros.). Director, Lloyd Bacon. Cast included: Frank McHugh, Pat O'Brien, and Gloria Stuart. Screenplay, Earl Baldwin and Ben Markson; from a story by Markson.

With Allen Jenkins in *The St. Louis Kid* (1934).

1934 **THE ST. LOUIS KID** (Warner Bros.). Director, Ray Enright. Cast included: Robert Barrat, Patricia Ellis, and Allen Jenkins. Screenplay, Warren Duff and Seton I. Miller; based on a story by Frederick Hazlitt Brennan.

1935 **DEVIL DOGS OF THE AIR** (Warner Bros.). Director, Lloyd Bacon. Cast included: Margaret Lindsay, Helen Lowell, Allen Jenkins, Frank McHugh, and Pat O'Brien. Screenplay, Earl Baldwin and Malcolm Stuart Boylan; taken from a story by John Monk Saunders.

As Tommy O'Toole in *Devil Dogs of the Air* (1935).

1935 **G MEN** (Warner Bros.). Director, William Reighley. Cast included: Robert Armstrong, Ann Dvorak, Margaret Lindsay, Barton MacLane, and Lloyd Nolan. Screenplay, Seton I. Miller; adapted from a story by Gregory Rogers.

With Margaret Lindsay in *G-Men* (1935).

As Bottom in *A Midsummer Night's Dream* (1935).

With Margaret Lindsay in *Frisco Kid* (1935).

With Mary Gordon in *The Irish in Us* (1935).

1935 **A MIDSUMMER NIGHT'S DREAM** (Warner Bros.). Directors, William Dieterle and Max Reinhardt. Cast included: Joe E. Brown, Olivia de Havilland, Hugh Herbert, Victor Jory, Frank McHugh, Jean Muir, Dick Powell, and Mickey Rooney. Screenplay, Charles Kenyon and Mary McCall, Jr.; based on the play by William Shakespeare.

1935 **THE IRISH IN US** (Warner Bros.). Director, Lloyd Bacon. Cast included: Olivia de Havilland, Allen Jenkins, Frank McHugh, and Pat O'Brien. Screenplay, Earl Baldwin; from a story by Frank Orsatti.

1935 **FRISCO KID** (Warner Bros.). Director, Lloyd Bacon. Cast included: Ricardo Cortez, Lily Damita, Margaret Lindsay, and Barton MacLane. Screenplay, Warren Duff and Seton I. Miller; based on a story by Duff and Miller.

With Stuart Erwin (l.) and June Travis in *Ceiling Zero* (1935).

(Below Left) With Edward Gargan (c.r.) in *Great Guy* (1936).

With Johnny Arthur (r.) in *Something to Sing About* (1937).

1935 **CEILING ZERO** (Warner Bros.). Director, Howard Hawks. Cast included: Stuart Erwin, Pat O'Brien, and June Travis. Screenplay, Frank Wead; based on a play by Wead.

1936 **GREAT GUY** (Grand Natural). Director, John G. Blystone. Cast included: Edward Brophy, James Burke, and Mae Clarke. Screenplay, James Edward Grant, Henry Johnson, Henry McCarty, and Harry Ruskin; from stories by Grant.

1937 **SOMETHING TO SING ABOUT** (Grand National). Director, Victor Schertzinger. Cast included: Mona Barrie, Evelyn Paw, William Frawley, and Gene Lockhart. Screenplay, Austin Parker; adapted from a story by Shertzinger.

(Above) With Pat O'Brien (c.l.) Ralph Bellamy (c.r.), and Marie Wilson in *Boy Meets Girl* (1938).

1938 **BOY MEETS GIRL** (Warner Bros.). Director, Lloyd Bacon. Cast included: Ralph Bellamy, Dick Foran, Frank McHugh, Pat O'Brien, and Marie Wilson. Screenplay, Bella and Sam Spewacks; from a play by the Spewacks.

(Left) As Rocky Sullivan in *Angels With Dirty Faces* (1938).

1938 **ANGELS WITH DIRTY FACES** (Warner Bros.). Director, Michael Curtiz. Cast included: George Bancroft, Humphrey Bogart, the Dead End Kids, Pat O'Brien, and Ann Sheridan. Screenplay, Warren Duff and John Wexley; based on a story by Rowland Brown.

As Jim Kincard in *The Oklahoma Kid* (1939).

1939 THE OKLAHOMA KID (Warner Bros.). Director, Lloyd Bacon. Cast included: Humphrey Bogart, Donald Crisp, and Rosemary Lane. Screenplay, Robert Buckner, Warren Duff, and Edward E. Paramore; adapted from a story by Wally Klein and Paramore.

With Stanley Ridges (l.) and Maxie Rosenbloom (r.) in *Each Dawn I Die* (1939).

1939 **THE ROARING TWENTIES** (Warner Bros.). Director, Raoul Walsh. Cast included: Humphrey Bogart, Gladys George, Priscilla Lane, Jeffrey Lynn, and Frank McHugh. Screenplay, Richard Macaulay, Robert Rossen, and Jerry Wald; adapted from a story by Mark Hellinger.

1939 **EACH DAWN I DIE** (Warner Bros.). Director, William Keighley. Cast included: George Bancroft, Jane Bryan, Victor Jory, George Raft, and Maxie Rosenbloom. Screenplay, Warren Duff and Norman Reilly Raine; based on a novel by Jerome Odlum.

1940 **THE FIGHTING 69TH** (Warner Bros.). Director, William Keighley. Cast included: George Brent, Tommy Dugan, Dick Foran, Alan Hale, Jr., Jeffrey Lynn, Frank McHugh, and Pat O'Brien. Screenplay, Dean Franklin, Fred Niblo, Jr., and Norman Reilly Raine.

With Frank McHugh (l.) and Humphrey Bogart (r.) in *The Roaring Twenties* (1939).

With Alan Hale in *The Fighting 69th* (1940).

With Ann Sheridan and Andy Devine (c.) in *Torrid Zone* (1940).

(Below) With Ann Sheridan in *City For Conquest* (1941).

1940 **TORRID ZONE** (Warner Bros.). Director, William Keighley. Cast included: Andy Devine, Pat O'Brien, Ann Sheridan and Helen Vinson. Screenplay, Richard Macaulay and Jerry Wald.

1941 **CITY FOR CONQUEST** (Warner Bros.). Director, Anatale Litvak. Cast included: Frank Craven, Donald Crisp, Elia Kazan, Arthur Kennedy, Frank McHugh, Anthony Quinn, and Ann Sheridan. Screenplay, John Wexley; taken from a novel by Aben Kandel.

1941 **THE STRAWBERRY BLONDE** (Warner Bros.). Director, Raoul Walsh. Cast included: Jack Carson, Alan Hale, Olivia de Havilland, Rita Hayworth, and George Tobias. Screenplay, Julius and Philip Epstein; based on a play by James Hagan.

With Rita Hayworth in *The Strawberry Blonde* (1941).

With Jack Carson (l.), Bette Davis, and Stuart Erwin (r.) in
The Bride Came C.O.D. (1941).

1941 **THE BRIDE CAME C.O.D.** (Warner Bros.). Director,
William Keighley. Cast included: Jack Carson, Bette
Davis, Stuart Erwin, and George Tobias. Screenplay,
Julius and Philip Epstein; from a story by Kenneth Earl
and M.M. Musselman.

1942 **CAPTAINS OF THE CLOUDS** (Warner Bros.). Direc-
tor, Michael Curtiz. Cast included: Alan Hale, Brenda
Marshall, Dennis Morgan, and George Tobias. Screen-
play, Arthur T. Horman, Richard Macauley, and Norman
Reilly Raine; adapted from a story by Roland Gillett and
Horman.

144

1942 **YANKEE DOODLE DANDY** (Warner Bros.). Director, Michael Curtiz. Cast included: Jeanne Cagney, Rosemary DeCamp, Walter Huston, Joan Leslie, Irene Manning S.Z. Sakall, George Tobias, and Richard Whorf. Screenplay, Robert Buckner and Edmund Joseph; from a story by Buckner.

1943 **JOHNNY COME LATELY** (United Artists). Director, William K. Howard. Cast included: Grace George, Hattie McDaniel, Edward McNamara, and Marjorie Main. Screenplay, John Van Druten; based on a novel by Louis Bromfield.

With Dennis Morgan in *Captains of the Clouds* (1942).

With S. Z. Sakall in *Yankee Doodle Dandy* (1942).

As Tom Richards in *Johnny Come Lately* (1943).

With Jeanne Cagney and William Bendix ( ) in *The Time of Your Life* (1948).

(Left) With Sylvia Sidney in *Blood on the Sun* (1945).

1943 BLOOD ON THE SUN (United Artists), Director, Frank Lloyd. Cast included: Robert Armstrong, Rosemary DeCamp, Wallace Ford, and Sylvia Sidney. Screenplay, Lester Cole; adapted from a story by Garrett Ford.

(Below Left) As Bob Sharkey in *13 Rue Madeleine* (1946).

1946 13 RUE MADELEINE (Twentieth Century-Fox). Director, Henry Hathaway. Cast included: Walter Abel, Annabella, Richard Conte, Sam Jaffe, and Frank Lattimore. Screenplay, Sy Bartlett and John Monks, Jr.

1948 THE TIME OF YOUR LIFE (United Artists). Director, H.C. Potter. Cast included: James Barton, William Bendix, Ward Bond, Jeanne Cagney, Broderick Crawford, Paul Draper, and Wayne Morris. Screenplay, Nathaniel Curtis, from the play by William Saroyan.

1949 WHITE HEAT (Warner Bros.). Director, Raoul Walsh. Cast included: Steve Cochran, Virginia Mayo, Edmond O'Brien, and Margaret Wycherly, Screenplay, Ivan Goff and Ben Roberts; based on a story by Virginia Kellogg.

With Virginia Mayo in *White Heat* (1949).

With Alan Hale, Jr., in *The West Point Story* (1950).

740-10

With Barbara Payton in *Kiss Tomorrow Goodbye* (1950).

1950 **THE WEST POINT STORY** (Warner Bros.). Director, Roy Del Ruth, Cast included: Doris Day, Alan Hale, Jr., Gordon MacRae, Virginia Mayo, Gene Nelson, and Roland Winters. Screenplay, Charles Hoffman, John Monks, Jr., and Irving Wallace; from a story by Wallace.

1950 **KISS TOMORROW GOODBYE** (Warner Bros.). Director, Gordon Douglas. Cast included: Luther Adler, Ward Bond, Steve Brodie, Helena Carter, William Frawley, Matt McHugh, and Barbara Payton. Screenplay, Harry Brown; adapted from a novel by Horace McCoy.

With Selena Royle (l.), Raymond Massey (c.), and Gig Young (r.) in *Come Fill the Cup* (1951).

1951 **COME FILL THE CUP** (Warner Bros.). Director, Gordon Douglas. Cast included: James Gleason, Sheldon Leonard, Raymond Massey, Phyllis Thaxter, and Gig Young. Screenplay, Ivan Goff and Ben Roberts; based on a novel by Harlan Ware.

1952 **WHAT PRICE GLORY** (Twentieth Century-Fox).
Director, John Ford. Cast included: Corinne Calvert, Dan
Dailey, William Demarest, Craig Hill, and Robert Wagner.
Screenplay, Henry and Phoebe Ephron; from the play by
Maxwell Anderson and Laurence Stallings.

(Above) With Corinne Calvet and Dan Dailey in *What Price Glory?* (1952).

(Right) With John Derek (l.) in *Run for Cover* (1955).

With Barbara Hale in *A Lion in the Streets* (1953).

1953 **A LION IS IN THE STREETS** (Warner Bros.). Director, Raoul Walsh. Cast included: Warner Anderson, Jeanne Cagney, Anne Francis, Barbara Hale, and Frank McHugh. Screenplay, Luther Davis; based on a novel by Adria Locke Langley.

1955 **RUN FOR COVER** (Paramount). Director, Nicholas Ray. Cast included: John Derek, Jean Hersholt, Viveca Lindfors, and Grant Withers. Screenplay, Winston Miller; from a story by Harriet Frank, Jr., and Irving Ravetch.

With Doris Day in *Love Me Leave Me* (1955).

1955 **LOVE ME OR LEAVE ME** (MGM). Director, Charles Vidor. Cast included: Harry Bellaver, Doris Day, Robert Keith, Cameron Mitchell, and Tom Tully. Screenplay, Daniel Fuchs and Isobel Lennart; adapted from a story by Fuchs.

(Below) With Bob Hope (l.) in *The Seven Little Foys* (1955).

(Above) With Henry Fonda (r.) in *Mister Roberts* (1955).

1955 **MISTER ROBERTS** (Warner Bros.). Directors, Mervyn Le Roy, John Ford, Cast included: Ward Bond, Henry Fonda, Jack Lemmon, Betsy Palmer and William Powell. Screenplay, Joshua Logan and Frank Nugent, from the play by Thomas Heggen and Logan.

1955 **THE SEVEN LITTLE FOYS** (Paramount). Director, Melville Shavelson. Cast included: Bob Hope, George Tobias, and Milly Vitale. Screenplay, Jack Rose and Melville Shavelson.

With Irene Papas in *Tribute to a Bad Man* (1956).

(Right) With Barbara Stanwyck (c.) and Betty Lou Keim in *These Wilder Years* (1956).

1956 **TRIBUTE TO A BAD MAN** (MGM). Director, Robert Wise. Cast included: Don Dubbins, Stephan McNally, Vic Morrow and Irene Papas. Screenplay, Michael Blankfort; based on a story by Jack Schaefer.

1956 **THE WILDER YEARS** (MGM). Director, Roy Rowland. Cast included: Edward Andrews, Don Dubbins, Betty Lou Keim, Walter Pidgeon and Barbara Stanwyck. Screenplay, Frank Fenton; adapted from a story by Ralph Wheelwright.

(Left) As Lon Chaney, Sr., in *Man of a Thousand Faces* (1957).

With Shirley Jones in *Never Steal Anything Small* (1958).

1957 **MAN OF A THOUSAND FACES** (Universal-International). Director, Joseph Pevney. Cast included: Jim Backus, Jane Greer, Dorothy Malone and Marjorie Rambeau. Screenplay, R. Wright Campbell, Ivan Goff and Ben Roberts; taken from a story by Ralph Wheelwright.

1959 **NEVER STEAL ANYTHING SMALL** (Universal-International). Director, Charles Lederer. Cast included: Shirley Jones, Nehemiah Persoff, Roger Smith and Cara Williams. Screenplay, Charles Lederer; based on a play by Maxwell Anderson and Rouben Mamoulian.

(Left) With Don Murray in *Shake Hands with the Devil* (1959).

As Fleet Admiral William "Bull" Halsey in *The Gallant Hours* (1960).

1959 **SHAKE HANDS WITH THE DEVIL** (United Artists). Director, Michael Anderson. Cast included: Cyril Cusack, Glynis Johns, Don Murray, Michael Redgrave, Sybil Thorndike and Dana Wynter. Screenplay, Ivan Goff and Ben Roberts; based on a novel by Reardon Conner.

1960 **THE GALLANT HOURS** (United Artists). Director, Robert Montgomery. Cast included: Ward Costello, Richard Jaeckel, Karl Swenson and Dennis Weaver. Screenplay, Frank D. Gilroy and Beirne Lay.

With Lilo Pulver and Hanns Lothar (r.) in *One, Two, Three* (1961).

1961 **ONE, TWO, THREE** (United Artists). Director, Billy Wilder. Cast included: Horst Buchholz, Arlene Francis, Lilo Pulver and Pamela Tiffin. Screenplay, I.A.L. Diamond and Wilder; from a play by Ferene Molnar.